salt and ink

Krista Kulisch

Presentation by *BookLeaf Publishing*

Web: www.bookleafpub.com

E-mail: info@bookleafpub.com

ISBN: 9789357212021

First edition 2023

fairy tale

the soles of shoes
front porch and my eyes
move one
foot after
this picture
after effects
prodding pushing
the gnashing of bristles
afterthoughts

two whole hands, mommy

the dark trail
woods
halfway down
leaves cold
wet quiet under
breadcrumbs
inside
stew over fire

she was not tending to me.

summer swimming

velvet wafts of stale air
chewed gum melted into sinking
pools for unsuspecting strays
who don't watch the hands
of the clock tick tick ticking
drops from the small pointed
number three erasing the weave of
the vacuumed rug crunch
of tires rolling over gum
hot breath claws its
way to the surface of a tight
throat

they say you cannot trust
the memories of children

molded clay of context
charades and hide and
seek monsters pulling you by your
kneecaps to the darkness between
the bed and the wall scratched
with hash marks to count
down keep track
ignore and remember
smeared windowed stories

sticky splayed hands hold
evidence in dismembered increments
between hips
pelvis
wings
call it growing pains

you cannot trust
the memories of children
when you don't know
where you buried them

diving into a blanket
of heat and bodies seared
with invisible ink i
float into the deep
end sit criss cross
applesauce
claim fistfuls of water
fumble and
shovel
wrists under
my knees an anchor
watch the screams bubble
to the surface
with alarming
calm

ars poetica

write with blood
open-veined in salt air
driftwood picnics
planks hard and dry
this feast of words to
keep you afloat
fingers produce ink and salt
to form all of the words
you dare not
say

taste
one of these
sunbaked shriveled
letters scattered before you
tell me
what color do you smell
as you gnash it
with your wet and sticky teeth
into pulp
or fiction

wrap a word around your finger
twist it tight
run into the waves

pulling the tie
that binds
behind you above you around you
dive into the churning foam
as words trail you
from above signal
to the others that
you are
swimming
alone

december 92

wet sun on concrete
glaring winter dark lipstick
stained jewel panels

they bend with small smiles
lower their eyes with a nod
hands pressed on shoulders

hymns whispered in sync
a gentle breeze blows outside
a hallelujah

the mourning dove sings
the prayer through the branches
rippling and rustling

tomorrow the ground
will be warm and dry again
you will still sleep long

a toast

here's to the girl with the glass blown eyes
the lover of time wasted
dirty bedsheets and empty wine
and here's to the lady with the washed and set
hair
antique suitcases eaten away
pay rides at the fair
lies we tell ourselves reflect over windows
cast fluorescent shadows
we pretend we've always known
just between you and i and this pen feels heavy
i don't know why he stays
but i know why i'm me
here's to the guy who breathes his desperation
sings his exhalation
denies his expectation
and here's to the guy that's never really aware
hands his wants blindly
to the girls with blank stares
the firefly is only so bright as the bottle that
captures her
beating wings in a fury
captivity always causes a stir

elegy for my brother at sea

it was a ring
no machine
tearing around
the corner to catch it
you expiring politely
hours earlier
a december gust
air cradling
you bobbing
up and down
i saw it

i know what you meant to do
wrenched
my hair from its
stem to the
back of the plot
replanted roots into
preconceived notions
hung like cuticles
crescent moons
smoked fish
handheld video cameras
a doberman
leashed and barking

you found yourself
screaming mayday
empty vessel suspended
on the downward west-
facing slope
poke and stick
ink of a lovesick
boy next
to the other side of
fear the rest
is yours

for the birds

your truth smells
like metal
hammered over time
worn with
pride by soldiers
fighting out of
habit for reasons
they can't explain
your laughter looks
like glass
reflecting my own
defenses
in the morning light
i recognize that smile
have used it myself
on more
than one occasion
you have a lot of space to fill
between the land
mines exploding around
you
time to kill
in these moments
you've held onto
if i could

give you my
eyes
next time you look
the mirror
would surprise
with what you see

floating

you were my first
and only shot
at something real
i took for granted
the life preserver
you threw would stay
attached
to you
somehow
disregarded the
fact that every
search and
rescue team
calls it a day
at some point
buries the memory
of a body
moves on
i've run out
of flares
striking them blindly
at the first sight of land
never realizing
until now
that you were waiting

right where i left you
never realizing
until now
that you might someday
drift away

fresh eyes in the morning

hungover and bloated
like a sewer fish on the moist concrete
bright with the smell of fear
this self imposed exile
feels heavy dripping off my skin
escaping out of pores
sticky and thirsty
i'm growing weary with all
my projections
cultivating a garden of myself
in a caked down tangle of weeds
beneath a rustic metal fence
staring at rendered images in
glossy magazines
smudging the wine glass
with the grease of my longing
the dampness clings to the every
nerve ending
my insides crowded and pushing
against each other
craving fresh air and pure water
knowing the grass is greener
but on the other side of what

you belong to me too

i awoke to find anger asleep on my pillow
she must have crawled in when i was dreaming

i invented you
out of stolen cigarettes, unnoticed rebellion,
and a trash compactor

you invented me
out of dried leaves, the ocean's redemption,
and a knife

it was supposed to be make believe
but i recognized you
and you recognized me

there is a lake where
who we are and who we want to be meet
it is stagnant with the decay
of too many bodies
fighting for the same air

we're buried there

i woke up on the pillow where you memory sits
holding my breath

so i wouldn't disturb you
by the time i blinked
you had disappeared
i walked the dogs
made some coffee
and wished i never knew you

i've traded your secrets for momentary empathy

i woke up yesterday and found myself
asleep in the warm cloud of your memory
it rolled me through my day
i drank coffee at 8:16am
and for a moment i thought
you were on your way over
until i remembered
i knew you in a past life
you don't exist in this new one
i would have cried
but i've forgotten how
so i took a walk a drive a break
and did something you
wouldn't recognize
i forgot about you

you are here

i hated myself
when i was with you
but at least
i knew who i was
your presence alone
gave me a reason
to crawl inside
the skin and bones
into the heart
of the matter
your perception
gave me a reason to fight
to strive
to be something
different
something more
my response to your anger
heavy as chains
the strength
i used to escape
the answer to the riddle
however,
i didn't go as planned
instead of running
into the forest

i stood in the clearing
while wild brush
and trees rooted
themselves around me
i kept my eyes shut tight
never noticing
i didn't move
for years
the life i though
would find me
disappeared
and left me alone
again
still not knowing
which way to run
now so disoriented
i can't even remember
which direction
i started from
my compass points
lack reference
the stars don't tell
which way to head
my feet are planted
while my mind races
against an enemy
i dont' even recognize
anymore
i almost wish

you'd find me again
so i'd have
a demon to fight
other than myself

trainwreck

i was the accident
you paused to look at
on your way home
you shouldn't have pulled over
the shoulder is too dangerous
treacherous place to land
especially when it's broken
i would have been safer
relying on the kindness
of strangers
i would have been safer
relying on myself
insteadn
i dug a hole
while you sifted through
the wreckage looking
for pieces that fit
gluing your perception
into an image
i didn't recognize
it was a photoshopped replica
of a girl i once knew
missing the one element
that would have made me whole
i still haven't found it

but i refuse
i repeat i refuse
to revisit the site of you
saving me

status update

i found your anxiety
tucked into the pages of a book
i always meant to read
until something else came up
i saw your eyes
in the bottom of my wine glass
so i opened another bottle
and filled it to the rim
i smelled your skin
in the back of my throat
so i changed my clothes
and brushed and flossed twice
i misplaced your apology
somewhere in my ribcage
all that blood and oxygen
hide evidence well

it hasn't been going well
this letting go of you

sleepwalk

i used to think i knew you better
than the rest would wake to
find you watching me dream believing
i was finally safe to be
me free to unleash the ugly
parts into the dark
comfort of pillows you
proved you could handle every
time i allowed a crack to shatter my
preconceived notions about love
relationships and my ability to
care you put your finger over my
lips to quiet my retreat i find
myself still holding my breath i
know once i exhale i won't smell
you anymore

self-reflection

forgotten deadlines misplaced
anxiety fawning innocence forced
epiphanies throwing my words
up into a crystalline bubble of drugstore
dish soap eager to point
out the beauty of something so
ordinary

self-medication unrequited
hope dimestore extravagance muddled
clarity an only child amid a fistful of
siblings waving my white flag in
a room full of
strangers

meaningless physicality deadpan
profoundness unbridled inferiority
uncomfortable
familiarity feeling helpless
when you tug at the
corners of the rug beneath my chipped
toenails

one way ticket

arrogance and hope
gloves i've stuffed my hands into
even though its warm outside
funny how time
changes the shape of things
the distance between us
is the mold i use
to visualize the shape of my heart
it's grown dusty and faded
it smells like bruised skin
has forgotten the
context of the wounds
i was the accident you paused
to look at on your way home
you shouldn't have pulled over
the shoulder is a dangerous
treacherous place to land
i worry that returning
to battlefields
already conquered
will awaken my shadow
in a room with no light
the equivalent of searching
an empty ashtray
for something in inhale

my words wet matches
i would sleep easier
if i believe you never loved me
rather
i've acquired the burden
of hindsight
heavy like freedom
watching you gather leftovers
front the wreckage
looking for pieces that fit
gluing your perception
into an image i don't recognize
i spend evenings crawling
into the bottom of a wineglass
i had everything
i said i wanted
even packed it with me
when i left
oblivious to the fact
that my grip on
the fairy tale
would keep me from noticing
you walking away
and moving on

mixed signals

chipped toenails in fishnet stockings
feigning innocence on the bathroom floor
you taste of dead batteries
you smell of dead skin
forced smiles lighting the
darkened hallways

you were in my dream last night
crystal clear in a faded background
of another woman's life
your eyes wandered as i watched you
in the haze of lazy smoke
the words elude me
in my consciousness
you were looking for me
images unfurling in front of her
pictures she doesn't recognize
familiar yet strangely foreign

i try to write you into a pretty little sonnet
so that i can read you out loud
absorb your phonetics and
fade into your sounds
my memories are subjective
i remember what i want and

forgot the truth because
its easier to look in the mirror that way

misplaced honesty

pencil broke this
morning to use a pen and
you stained green
thought you were gold
you rusted through sitting
in the casino gambling away promises
i can't afford trying to fold
hands trembling jeans
ripped toes cold
murder of something up
your sleeve bleeding down the prints
of your feet small
talk aimed the cushion
the floor my mother cried at
the hospital door sitting on
the brink of
your laughter calling out numbers as
though the sums matter misplaced
honesty is always a phone
call away

incongruity

this is my dream broken
mirrors reflecting my
body a kaleidoscope lacking
geometry desires an exhale
crystalized in winter air tangible
real disappearing into fragments
of starlight for a moment
i saw you smiling looking
at me or through me i'm not
sure which these windows look
like walls when the sun is
sleeping every pumpkin has
an expression if lit
properly my carriage wheels
square artistic don't quite
work as they should form
follows function follows storm into
eye of the hurricane silent
utterly still watching the world
shift around me
this is my dream come true

moving on

i wrote your story this morning
on the palm of my hand
then folded my cards over my ribcage
in the shape of a white flag
fading in the distance

i no longer trust my eyesight
in daylight and well lit rooms
i left my fingerprints
on the side of the fireplace
back when i still believed in santa claus

i am the pink elephant standing
in your living room
or is it white
i want to get it right
see i know how important color is

red is anger sometimes love
blue is sadness and bruised skin
yellow is a coward unless it's a flower
then it's friendship
you can see how i might get confused

you seem shorter these days

ever since i tripped over my words
and inadvertently knocked over
the pedestal i built for you
shorter than me in bare feet even

you once spoke to me of truth and ignorance
as though exclusive of one another
as though i needed to be taught
but you spoke in tongues over coffee
diluted your intentions with sugar
and room temperature cream

so i wrapped your words in a doggy bag
in case you're hungry later
and need a snack
i haven't heard your voice in weeks
you choose your silence well

it speaks volumes on dusty shelves
smudging my skin with the ink of
important death and genocide
text so permanent
it ignites wood and protects dishes
every time my lease is up